CAPTURED
TELEVISION
HISTORY

TV SHAPES PRESIDENTIAL POLITICS
IN THE KENNEDY-NIXON DEBATES

T0053051

by Michael Burgan

Content Adviser: Alan Schroeder
Professor, School of Journalism
Northeastern University

COMPASS POINT BOOKS
a capstone imprint

Compass Point Books are published by Capstone Press,
1710 Roe Crest Drive, North Mankato, Minnesota 56003
www.mycapstone.com

Editorial Credits
Michelle Bisson, editor; Tracy McCabe, designer; Svetlana Zhurkin, media researcher;
Kathy McColley, production specialist; Library Consultant: Kathleen Baxter

Photo Credits
AP Photo: 19, Jackie Johnston, cover; Franklin D. Roosevelt Library and Museum,
18, 57; Getty Images: Bettmann, 5, 8, 13, 16, 36, 48–49, 56 (left), CBS Photo
Archive, 6, 12, 30, Lambert, 9, Popperfoto, 39, The Boston Globe/Dan Goshtigian,
20, The LIFE Picture Collection/Dirck Halstead, 50, 58, The LIFE Picture Collection/
Ed Clark, 29, The LIFE Picture Collection/George Silk, 11, 56 (right), The LIFE Picture
Collection/Paul Schutzer, 35, The LIFE Picture Collection/Robert W. Kelley, 24–25,
The LIFE Picture Collection/Steve Liss, 55; Newscom: CNP/Arnie Sachs, 41, Everett
Collection, 43, UPI/Kevin Dietsch, 53, 59 (bottom), Zuma Press/Arthur Grace, 46,
47, 59 (top); Shutterstock: Everett Historical, 23

Library of Congress Cataloging-in-Publication Data
Cataloging-in-publication information is on file with the Library of Congress.
ISBN 978-0-7565-5823-9 (library binding)
ISBN 978-0-7565-5827-7 (paperback)
ISBN 978-0-7565-5831-4 (ebook pdf)

TABLEOFCONTENTS

Chapter One

PREPARING FOR THE GREAT DEBATE

At 7:30 p.m. on September 26, 1960, a large car pulled up to WBBM, a Chicago television station. Inside was Richard M. Nixon, the vice president of the United States. Nixon, a Republican, had served almost eight years in that role, alongside President Dwight D. Eisenhower. Now Nixon was running for president himself. In an hour, he would face his opponent in the race, Democratic Senator John F. Kennedy of Massachusetts. The two men had agreed to hold the first-ever televised debates between two U.S. presidential candidates.

When Nixon stepped out of the car, people noticed immediately that he didn't look well. Just two weeks before, he had left the hospital after being treated for a knee infection. The hospital stay prevented him from campaigning for almost two weeks. Meanwhile, Kennedy had continued to travel across the country, trying to win the support of American voters. When Nixon left the hospital, he felt pressure to follow what he later called "a brutal schedule," as he tried to make up for the time he had lost. He visited 25 states and traveled 25,000 miles (40,235 km) in the days leading up to the debate in Chicago.

The hospital stay and the travel left Nixon thin and looking tired. To add to his woes, as he left the

Senators John F. Kennedy (left) and Richard M. Nixon shook hands before engaging in a debate that would change how U.S. presidential elections are fought.

car he banged the knee that had been infected. And he had a fever. An official from one of the three TV networks broadcasting the debates asked him, "How do you feel?" Nixon replied, "Not so well." The official asked if Nixon wanted to cancel the first debate, but the vice president said no.

Minutes later, another car pulled up to the TV studio. Out stepped Kennedy, looking fit and tan.

Producers Frank Stanton (standing, at right) and Don Hewitt watched the first televised presidential debate along with the rest of the nation.

He had been campaigning in sunny California, and one observer said the tan and Kennedy's youthful appearance made him look like a movie star. Nixon was only a few years older than him, but Kennedy seemed much younger. In the weeks before the debate, one of Nixon's aides suggested he use a sun lamp to get a tan too, but he had refused. Kennedy knew that the presidential debates would give him a chance to reach millions of American voters at once.

Kennedy came from a wealthy Massachusetts family. Joseph Kennedy, his father, was determined to use his fortune to help his son get elected president. John was elected to the House of Representatives as a Democrat in 1946, representing part of Boston. He won his Senate seat in 1952. Four years later, he was in the running to be the Democratic Party's candidate for vice president, but he lost to Senator Estes Kefauver at the convention. The convention was televised, and Kennedy gave his first national TV speech during it, though he had appeared on several news shows before then. Despite his rise in national politics during the 1950s, Kennedy was not well known across the country when he announced he was running for president in 1960. The televised debates with Nixon would help him explain to voters in all 50 states his policies and plans.

The popularity of television had exploded during the 1950s. In 1946 just several thousand U.S. homes owned TVs. Less than 10 years later more than half of the country's homes owned at least one set and by 1960 the number was about 90 percent. The programming was only in black and white, and people relied on antennas to receive the TV signal. Only three networks broadcast across the country, limiting what people could watch. But in the decades before the development of the Internet, television was the major source of entertainment and news for millions of Americans.

VIDEO AND THE CATHOLIC QUESTION

John F. Kennedy took questions from the Protestant religious leaders in the audience.

Knowing how important video was becoming in politics, Kennedy used it to address a major problem he faced. Before 1960 no member of the Roman Catholic Church had ever been elected president of the United States. In parts of the country, some Protestants believed that a Catholic president would follow the orders of the pope, the head of Roman Catholicism, rather than always do what was best for most Americans. To address this fear, Kennedy gave a speech in Houston on September 12, 1960, before a group of mostly Protestant religious leaders. The speech was also televised across Texas. Kennedy assured viewers he would always put the interests of the country above his religion.

On public matters, he said, "the church does not speak for me." Kennedy then made video copies of the speech and sent them to local TV stations across the country. Some showed the full speech, while others just broadcast highlights. Kennedy wanted Americans to hear his message of the need to tolerate all religions, and that he would not put his faith above his service as president. With his election, Kennedy was the first president who did not belong to a Protestant faith, and he remains the only Catholic president as of now.

Families in the 1950s usually owned one TV and watched it together.

Kennedy realized early on that TV would play a growing role in U.S. politics. Starting in 1957 he talked to media experts about how to present the best image on TV. He learned that how he looked was just as important as what he said. During the 1960 campaign, he bought his own portable video recorder to tape his public appearances. Video recorders had been invented only a few years before, and even most TV stations didn't have the portable machines because they were so expensive. By studying tapes of himself, Kennedy learned how to improve his speaking style. He believed that television favored younger candidates, like himself. Kennedy was 43 when the campaign began, which was young for a presidential candidate. He wrote in 1959 that youth "is definitely an asset in creating a television image that people like and (most difficult of all) remember."

Richard Nixon was no stranger to TV either. In 1948, while serving in the U.S. House of Representatives, he had taken part in televised hearings investigating the activities of Alger Hiss. A former government employee, Hiss had been accused of belonging to the Communist Party at a time when many Americans feared the rise of communism around the world. A speech Nixon made on television in 1952 helped him keep his spot on the Republican ticket as the vice presidential candidate. As vice president, Nixon often appeared on TV shows, and in 1959 he took part with Nikita Khrushchev in what was called the "kitchen debate." Khrushchev was the leader of the Soviet Union, the world's most powerful communist nation at the time. He and Nixon appeared together in a model U.S. kitchen that had been set up in the Soviet capital of Moscow. It was part of an event that highlighted U.S. products. Nixon and Khrushchev began to argue about the value of communism compared to the political and economic systems in the United States. The debate was taped and shown on U.S. television the next day.

But during the 1960 presidential campaign, Nixon was unsure at first whether or not to debate Kennedy.

He wrote in 1959 that youth "is definitely an asset in creating a television image that people like and (most difficult of all) remember."

THE CHECKERS SPEECH

Nixon's Checkers speech saved his political career.

Before 1960 Nixon's most famous television moment came in what is known today as the Checkers speech. During the 1952 presidential campaign some people thought Nixon had wrongly taken money donated by some of his supporters after he won a seat in the U.S. Senate in 1950. The money was to pay for some of his political expenses, and the fund was legal. But critics suggested that Nixon had spent the money on personal items, which he denied. Because of this Nixon was in danger of losing his position as Eisenhower's vice presidential candidate. On September 23 Nixon gave the first live political television speech ever broadcast across the U.S. In it, he asserted he had done nothing wrong and that he and his family were far from wealthy. He said the only personal gift he had gotten after the 1950 election was a cocker spaniel named Checkers. Nixon said his daughters loved Checkers, and he added, "I just want to say this, right now, that regardless of what [people] say about it, we're gonna keep it."

The Checkers speech led several million people across the country to send messages in support of Nixon, and he remained the Republican vice presidential candidate. In 1999 a poll of U.S. media experts ranked it one of the 10 most important speeches in U.S. history.

CBS producer
Don Hewitt talks
to Nixon before
the presidential
debate.

Eisenhower said he shouldn't. The president told
Nixon he would only give Kennedy extra attention
by participating in the debates. But Nixon worried
that Kennedy and others would criticize him if he
avoided the debates. Nixon later wrote, "I would have
opened myself up to the charge that I was afraid to
defend the Administration's and my own record."
And Nixon knew that most Americans wanted to see
the two men meet face to face. He also believed he
could make a better impression than Kennedy, since
he had taken part in debates through high school and
college.

As the first debate of September 26 drew near,

Kennedy and a campaign adviser confer with Hewitt about the set up of the debate.

the candidates prepared in different ways. Kennedy went to Chicago a few weeks early. He and his team stayed at the Ambassador East Hotel to prepare. He also met with Don Hewitt, who was going to direct the first debate for CBS, one of the three networks broadcasting the debates. Kennedy wanted to know where he and Nixon would stand and other details about the production of the first show. "He wanted to know everything," Hewitt later said. "Nixon I never saw until he arrived that night in the studio."

To be ready for any question, Kennedy took time whenever he could to study the issues the journalists at the debate might ask. Then, on the 26th, his aides played the role of the journalists asking questions, and Kennedy responded. Nixon chose to go over notes by himself that day, rather than pretending he was in an actual debate.

On the day before the first debate, Frank Stanton, the president of CBS, told *The New York Times* that the debates would change American politics. He believed that the candidates would be forced to more clearly state their views on important issues than ever before. Stanton also said the candidates "would be peeled down to the man himself," giving voters a better understanding of who Nixon and Kennedy were.

On the night of the 26th, after Kennedy arrived at WBBM, the two candidates shook hands in the TV studio where the debate would take place. Only they, the journalists taking part, and the TV crew were allowed in the studio. Several hundred reporters would have to watch the debate on TV screens in the building. Hewitt asked each man if he wanted makeup. Both said no, though later they had their own staff people apply a little. Nixon put on a product called Lazy Shave to try to hide his whiskers. Even after shaving, he knew his face could look dark. But the makeup he used made him look pale, so he looked even sicker. Hewitt was not sure Nixon looked his best. But Nixon's advisers were satisfied with his appearance. As 8:30 p.m. approached, the two candidates were ready to speak to millions of Americans and begin what the TV network called "the Great Debates."

Several hundred reporters would have to watch the debate on TV screens in the building.

ChapterTwo
THE PATH TO THE KENNEDY-NIXON DEBATES

More than a hundred years before the Great Debates of 1960, Abraham Lincoln took part in another series of debates that made history. When the 1960 debates began, many people referred back to those famous debates. Lincoln, though, was not running for president; he hoped to represent Illinois in the U.S. Senate. In an age before radio and television, only about 75,000 people actually saw and heard the two men speak. But the debates helped shape Lincoln's career as a politician on the rise..

In 1858 Lincoln faced the incumbent senator from Illinois, Stephen Douglas, in seven debates across their state. Like Kennedy, Lincoln was less well known than his opponent, so he was eager for the public to see him appear with Senator Douglas. And like Nixon, Douglas was not keen on debating Lincoln, but he didn't want voters to think he was scared to face him. For their debates, Lincoln and Douglas stood on a stage together. No newspaper writers asked questions. Instead, each man talked for up to 90 minutes at a time, focusing mostly on the most important issue of the day—slavery. In the end, Lincoln lost the election. But the debates won him national attention, since many newspapers reported

Slavery was the main focus of the 1858 debate between Lincoln and Douglas.

on them. Some newspapers published transcripts of the debates, so people could read exactly what Lincoln had said. In 1860, when he ran for president, Lincoln published a book with some of these newspaper reports. Even more people learned about him and where he stood on slavery.

Lincoln and Douglas followed a pattern that had emerged earlier during the 19th century. Two candidates running for state offices or Congress sometimes engaged in debates that voters could attend. Presidential candidates, however, did not meet in that way.

The ability of debaters to reach a large audience at one time had to wait until the invention of radio at the beginning of the 20th century. About 20 million Americans had access to radio broadcasts by the mid-1920s. In 1924 some tuned in to hear the Democratic and Republican parties choose their presidential candidates. It was the first time these political conventions were broadcast. In the years to come, both candidates and elected officials used radio to reach voters, though they did not hold debates.

Republican presidential candidate Wendell Wilkie tried to change that in 1940. He challenged President Franklin D. Roosevelt to a series of debates over the radio. The president, however, declined. As the incumbent, Roosevelt was better known than his challengers. Roosevelt did not want to do anything to help his opponent win attention from voters.

Eight years later, in 1948, two Republicans battling for their party's presidential nomination faced each other in a debate in Oregon that was broadcast over radio. Harold Stassen and Thomas Dewey debated the issue of outlawing communism in the United States. Each candidate spoke for 20 minutes on the topic and then had 8½ minutes to reply to the other's statement. No journalists took part. Newspapers did not see a clear winner of the debate. But one Washington, D.C., newspaper saw value in it. The *Star* wrote that debates between candidates revealed

THE FIRESIDE CHATS OF FDR

President Franklin Delano Roosevelt reached millions of people with his weekly radio chats and changed the way people thought of the president.

While Franklin Delano Roosevelt did not take part in a radio debate, he understood the value of radio for reaching voters. Shortly after he became president in 1933 Roosevelt made a national radio address to discuss his decision to shut down the country's banks for a short time. The U.S. was going through the Great Depression, which led some businesses to close and millions of Americans to lose their jobs. Many were rushing to take their money out of banks because they were afraid the banks would fail and they would lose their money. Roosevelt spoke to the country to try to calm people's fears about the problems they faced during the Great Depression. In the years that followed, Roosevelt gave almost 30 more of these addresses, which were nicknamed fireside chats. The president was not actually sitting by a cozy fire. But the name suggested that he was speaking informally and, most importantly, directly to the American people. Other presidents had spoken on the radio before, but they did not have a wide audience. By 1933 two-thirds of American homes had a radio. Roosevelt's chats reached millions of people at once in the days before television.

Harold Stassen (left) and Thomas Dewey shook hands before their radio debate.

weaknesses in their ideas that might not appear in a written speech. "If there were more of them," the newspaper continued, "we would have better campaigns, candidates better prepared to discuss the real issues of the day, and [voters] . . . better able to judge both issues and candidates."

In 1952 television played a major role in a presidential campaign for the first time. The networks broadcast both the Democratic and Republican conventions. Local stations also covered

political events throughout the year. For president, the Democrats chose Adlai Stevenson as their candidate, while the Republicans picked Dwight Eisenhower. Blair Moody, a U.S. senator from Michigan, suggested that the two candidates meet in a televised debate. Two of the three networks were ready to broadcast it but neither Stevenson nor Eisenhower wanted to take part. Eisenhower's strategy was simply to ignore Stevenson. He never said his name. Stevenson, for

Kennedy . . . saw that appearing on the same stage with the better-known candidate had been a boost.

his part, did not want to run the risk of coming off as weaker than his popular opponent.

One political debate did take place that year. John F. Kennedy was running for the U.S. Senate to represent Massachusetts. His opponent was Henry Cabot Lodge, who held the Senate seat Kennedy wanted. The debate was not televised, but the two candidates did appear together later on a national news show. On it, they discussed who would make a better president, Eisenhower or Stevenson. Kennedy won his election that year. He saw that appearing on the same stage with the better-known candidate had been a boost.

The idea of debates between presidential candidates came up again in 1956. A University of Maryland student named Fred Kahn wanted other students at his school to become more involved in politics. Kahn won some national attention when he suggested Eisenhower and his opponent, who again was Stevenson, debate at the school. University officials, however, withdrew their support for the debate, and neither candidate expressed interest in debating.

But Stevenson did take part in one televised debate that year. Before winning his party's nomination for president, Stevenson debated Estes Kefauver in Florida. At the time Kefauver was also seeking the Democratic presidential nomination.

Stevenson thought he could do well against Kefauver. The debate was shown on national TV. *The New York Times* described it as "an electronic innovation in political campaigning." The paper called it "an informal chat" rather than a real debate. In the future, though, the *Times* believed the format could produce meaningful political discussion between candidates of opposing parties.

By 1960 the idea of televising debates between the two presidential candidates had growing support. But the networks faced one major legal hurdle. A U.S. law regarding radio and TV broadcasts had a section that said networks must give equal time to all political candidates. According to Section 315, if the networks featured the Republican and Democratic presidential candidates on television for a debate, they had to give candidates from smaller parties the same amount of airtime. In any presidential campaign a number of people seek to run, even though they have almost no chance of winning. But the television networks felt it would not be practical to give all these lesser-known candidates equal time. And it would take up time given to commercial TV.

In 1956 the TV network NBC called on Congress to pass a law that would suspend Section 315 so it could broadcast presidential debates. But Congress did not act. In 1959 Congress did make it legal for TV networks to feature candidates on their news shows

But the television networks felt it would not be practical to give all these lesser-known candidates equal time.

THE FCC AND THE PUBLIC AIRWAVES

Many people in rural areas did not have TV sets but listened to news and debates on the radio.

Section 315 was one part of the Communication Act of 1934. Among other things, the act created the Federal Communications Commission (FCC). The FCC has the power to regulate how radio and television signals are broadcast through the air. Today, it also addresses issues relating to telephone, satellite, cable, and Internet communications. In the early days of radio, Congress wanted the government to regulate which companies broadcast and where. It also wanted some control over what was broadcast, since companies were using a resource that technically no one owned—the airwaves that carry electronic signals. TV and radio stations have to apply for a license to use a portion of the airwaves to transmit their signals. By 1934, with developments in TV taking place, the U.S. government

realized it needed an organization like the FCC to regulate all forms of communication. As the FCC defined it, Section 315 of the 1934 law meant anyone running for public office had to have equal access, which meant receiving equal airtime on radio and TV networks. Today, the FCC also regulates some of the political ads broadcasters can run during some campaigns. Qualified candidates for federal offices—president, vice president, and Congress—must be allowed to buy time to run their ads. But the stations have some control over when those ads can run. And groups that are promoting a particular issue rather than a candidate are not guaranteed that the right to buy airtime. In addition, all political ads must specify what person or group paid for them.

Politicians have been interviewed on *Meet the Press* for more than 60 years.

without offering equal time. With that change in the law, NBC offered to have the two major presidential candidates discuss issues on one of its news shows over a total of eight hours. Then Congress debated whether to suspend all the equal time requirements for the vice presidential and presidential races, but

only for 1960. While that debate went on, NBC invited Kennedy and Nixon to appear in a series of televised debates, which it called "the Great Debates." The other two networks made similar offers, and the candidates agreed to appear together on television. Congress suspended the equal time requirement in August, setting the stage for U.S. political history.

During the summer of 1960 representatives from the two candidates met with the television networks to set the number and format of the debates. An official from the Mutual Broadcasting System (MBS) also took part. MBS was the country's major radio network that was not owned by a TV network. It planned to air the debates too, as would the radio stations owned by the TV networks. Kennedy wanted five debates, while Nixon wanted three. The two men eventually agreed on four one-hour debates to take place from late September 26 to October 21, in advance of the November 8 election.

The two candidates also agreed to a format similar to what Stevenson and Kefauver had used in their 1956 TV appearance. It was a format common on some TV news programs of the era. (The best known of them, *Meet the Press*, still airs weekly.) Several journalists would ask questions, and the candidates would respond. They would be allowed to briefly comment on the other candidate's response. For two of the debates, each candidate would also make opening and closing statements. The format was not like a true debate, in which the debaters usually argue for or against a certain proposal. Both candidates rejected that type of debate, fearing the format might become too boring for the viewers. Questions from journalists meant the two candidates would have to be prepared to speak on a wide range of issues. Nixon and Kennedy agreed that the first debate would focus on domestic issues and the last one on international issues. The middle two would cover whatever topics the journalists chose. With the rules set, Kennedy and Nixon prepared to face off on live TV in front of millions of Americans.

With the rules set, Kennedy and Nixon prepared to face off on live TV in front of millions of Americans.

ChapterThree
THE FOUR GREAT DEBATES

On September 26, when the TV cameras went on in the studio of WBBM, they showed journalist Howard K. Smith sitting at a desk. On his right—to the viewers' left—sat Kennedy. On the other side of the desk was Nixon. The four journalists chosen to ask questions sat in front of the stage. They were not visible to the audience.

The background behind the candidates was gray. To make sure he stood out better against it, Kennedy wore a dark suit. Nixon, though, wore a gray one, and he seemed to almost blend into the background. One observer thought it also made him look paler than he already was. As historian W.J. Rorabaugh later wrote, Nixon seemed to fade away, while Kennedy popped out at the viewers. "Nixon probably lost the debate before it started," Rorabaugh said.

The lighting requests Nixon had made actually favored Kennedy's appearance. The debate was broadcast in black and white. To ensure the best picture quality for viewers, the CBS cameramen had to make some technical adjustments. Those led to greater contrast when the cameras turned to Kennedy, in turn making him look more appealing to viewers.

Smith began the broadcast by introducing the two candidates. Kennedy stood and gave the first opening statement, and although the debate was supposed to be about domestic issues, he talked first about the tensions in the world. Communism, he said, was moving parts of the world "in the direction of slavery." He said the United States must promote and defend freedom around the world, and while it was a great country, it could be better. At home, he said, the federal government had a role in helping people who needed it.

Nixon opened his statement by saying he agreed with Kennedy on certain points, but he disagreed with Kennedy's assessment of what the Eisenhower administration had accomplished. The country was hardly standing still, as Kennedy had often claimed. Under Republican leadership, Nixon said, the country had built more schools, hospitals, and highways than it had under President Harry Truman, a Democrat who held the office before Eisenhower. Workers were earning more money than during the Truman years and the cost of goods had gone down. Nixon said that he wanted to build on that record of Republican success.

Across the country, more than 73 million Americans watched some or all of this first Great Debate, while others listened on the radio. The camera usually focused on whoever was speaking. At times, though, director Hewitt chose to show the

Across the country, more than 73 million Americans watched some or all of this first Great Debate, while others listened on the radio.

The camera caught Nixon dabbing at sweat on his lip during the first debate.

reaction of one candidate while the other spoke. He later explained that he used these reaction shots at moments when he thought the television audience would want to see how one man was responding to the other's words. Kennedy appeared in several more of these reaction shots than Nixon. One reaction shot showed Nixon wiping sweat off his forehead, and at other times the camera showed him with sweat on his face. The hot lights in the studio caused him to sweat, but viewers might have seen it as a sign that he was nervous.

Kennedy (left) and Nixon on stage just before the start of the first debate.

After their opening statements, the candidates took questions from the journalists. They addressed such topics as aid to farmers, better medical care for the elderly, and the possibility of raising taxes. The journalists also brought up each candidate's experience, or lack of it. Nixon asserted that he had played a major role in advising Eisenhower on key issues. Kennedy noted that Lincoln had limited political experience when he was elected president in 1860.

When the hour ended, the two men posed for pictures with photographers. To reporters, neither candidate wanted to say who won. Kennedy, though, called the event "very useful," and Nixon complimented his opponent's performance. A Nixon aide, though, was quick to say that Nixon's team also thought he had done very well.

People all over the country had different reactions to the debate. Journalist Theodore White, who was covering the campaign, went the next day to a Kennedy speech in Ohio. He thought the audience there was more excited about Kennedy than earlier audiences had been, and White claimed it was because of the debate. Kennedy's appearance on TV, White wrote, "had given him a 'star quality' reserved only for television and movie idols." Ted Rogers, who had helped prepare Nixon for all his television appearances, thought the candidate's sickly look had definitely hurt him.

Political scientist Samuel Lubell had talked to voters across the country before the debate. Many of them had thought that Kennedy lacked the experience to be president. After the first debate, one Minnesota resident told Lubell, "I heard so much about Kennedy being inexperienced that I was surprised how well he did in the debate."

How people heard or watched the debate seemed to influence their reaction to some degree. Lyndon Johnson, Kennedy's vice presidential candidate, heard it on the radio and thought Nixon had won. But Henry Cabot Lodge, the Republican vice presidential candidate, watched it on TV and thought that Nixon's pale, sweaty appearance might have cost them the election. Frank Stanton of CBS was in the studio

"I heard so much about Kennedy being inexperienced that I was surprised how well he did in the debate."

watching the debate live. To him, Nixon "was on top of his subject a little better than Jack Kennedy was." But two polls of people who watched the debate on TV thought Kennedy had done a better job.

Nixon realized after the broadcast that his appearance had been a problem. His aides talked about his pale skin and the sweat on his face. One of his most trusted assistants was Rose Mary Woods. She gave an early indication of how poorly Nixon had looked on TV. She informed Nixon that her parents had watched and then called her to see if Nixon was sick. Nixon asked what she thought, and Woods had to agree. Nixon's mother, Hannah, watching in California, had the same concern. Later, Nixon admitted that he had not focused enough on his appearance. "I should have remembered that 'a picture is worth a thousand words.'" For his part,

THE DEBATE ON RADIO

While two polls showed that viewers who watched the debate on TV thought Kennedy had won, the result was different for people who listened to it on radio. Sindlinger & Company, a marketing firm, conducted a poll of people who listened to the first debate. They found that the radio listeners favored Nixon. For years, media experts thought this showed how vital television had been for Kennedy, and how much Nixon's appearance that night had hurt him. But in recent years, scholars have questioned the survey's accuracy. For one thing, Sindlinger questioned fewer than 300 people. For another, the company didn't consider whether the listeners favored one candidate or the other before the debate. The polls of TV watchers did take this into account. They showed that Kennedy was favored even by some people who originally supported Nixon. Finally, the radio survey did not account for the fact that most of the country owned TVs in 1960. People without TVs were more apt to be in poor, rural areas of the country. Voters in those regions tended to favor Republicans for president, and that preference may have influenced their views on the debate. Many were also Protestant and might have had questions about Kennedy's religion. Most historians now accept the idea that it was more than Kennedy's appearance that night on TV that helped him win the election.

Kennedy went to breakfast the next morning and told his aides, "Boy, did I nail him."

While many Americans focused on who won or lost the debate, some newspapers criticized the format. They would have preferred that the two men directly question each other. But some thought it was good television, if not exactly a real debate. The *St. Louis Dispatch* thought a "real discussion of the issues did take place." A reporter for *The New York Times* wrote, "The presence of both candidates on the same platform had an element of drama that simply could not be matched by a single nominee in the solo delivery of a speech." And at least one voter questioned by Lubell took comfort after watching the debate. Before watching, he said, he doubted either man was fit to be president. "But they both handled themselves well," he told Lubell. "The country will be secure with either man."

The debates were also shown in several foreign countries, including Canada and the United Kingdom. After the first debate, one London newspaper said it was "a brilliant lesson . . . on how to make an election come vividly alive." Another paper hoped that British politicians would take part in similar events on television. (In the decades that followed, other nations did televise debates between political candidates.)

Preparing for the next debate, on October 7 in Washington, D.C., Nixon knew he could not afford to look bad again. He began drinking four milkshakes a day to put on weight, and it worked. By October 7 he had gained 5 pounds (2.5 kg) and looked healthier. For the second debate, he also had makeup applied by a professional makeup artist and wore a darker suit. The focus for that debate would be more on the candidates' words than their looks. And Nixon could take some comfort in knowing that polls of likely voters indicated the race was still close. Kennedy had picked up some support since September 26, but not much.

For the second debate, neither candidate made an opening statement. Instead, they took turns answering questions from the four journalists there. The issues included relations with communist nations and the rights of black citizens in the United States. Afterward, Nixon received a much different response from his friends and supporters than after the first debate. There was no question that he had made a better impression this time. Several large newspapers also thought that Nixon had done better. One New York paper wrote, "The Vice President clearly won the second round." Private polling done for Kennedy showed that more people thought he had been more effective than Nixon during the second debate. But Nixon had closed the gap considerably, compared to the numbers after the first debate.

The third debate presented a technical challenge for ABC, the network in charge of televising it. Because of their schedules on October 13, Nixon was

"The Vice President clearly won the second round."

The candidates were in separate studios in different cities for their third debate.

in Los Angeles, while Kennedy was in New York. ABC had studios in each city. It built identical sets, so each man would be seen in front of the same background. It also worked hard on the technology. The long distances that the electronic signals had to travel could have made the sound and picture not quite match up. Adding to the problem, the signal carrying Kennedy's image and words had to travel twice as far as the one for Nixon. The signal for Kennedy was sent to Los Angeles, where it was mixed with one for Nixon. Then the combined signal was sent back to New York, where it was sent to other networks broadcasting the debate. Using special equipment, ABC made sure that Kennedy's words and images matched up.

Kennedy told
students at a Temple
University campaign
rally that he would
like a fifth debate.

Except for one brief split-screen shot, viewers
saw only one candidate at a time on their TV sets.
As with the second debate, Nixon and Kennedy took
questions from reporters without making opening
and closing statements. Nixon was upset with one
aspect of the debate. He thought that Kennedy broke
an agreement that the candidates could not use notes
on stage. Nixon saw that Kennedy brought papers
with him and looked down at one point to read a
quote. Nixon had called for no notes during the early
discussions over the debate formats. Kennedy and
his team insisted they had never agreed to Nixon's

Overall, as many as 90 percent of all Americans saw or listened to at least one of the debates.

request for no notes. The fourth debate, on October 21, drew the smallest audience. For that last debate, the two candidates discussed foreign policy.

For a time, the two candidates discussed adding a fifth debate. As before, Kennedy was eager to be on TV with Nixon as much as possible. Nixon thought it might be useful to have the two vice presidential candidates instead. The two sides tried to reach an agreement on a format, but in the end they chose not to have the fifth debate.

Overall, as many as 90 percent of all Americans saw or listened to at least one of the debates. With the last debate over, the two candidates continued to campaign across the country, hoping to win the support of undecided voters. Finally, on November 8, millions of Americans went to the polls to choose the next president.

Chapter Four

BEYOND THE GREAT DEBATES

When the votes were counted on Election Day, Kennedy barely beat Nixon in the popular vote. But presidents are actually chosen by the vote in the Electoral College, which is based on how many states a candidate wins. There, Kennedy won easily, taking 303 votes to Nixon's 219.

Experts tried to determine what role, if any, the Great Debates had played in Kennedy's victory. One poll showed that about half of the voters said the debates influenced their decision to some degree. About 3.4 million of the total 68.3 million voters said they based their vote solely on the candidates' debate performances. Of those people, about 75 percent said they voted for Kennedy. The newly elected president certainly thought the debates had helped him. On November 12, Kennedy said, "It was the TV more than anything else that turned the tide." Of course, Kennedy appeared on TV outside the debates. He went on news shows and paid for several hundred TV commercials. Some of them included video clips of the debates.

For his part, Nixon believed that many different factors led to his defeat, but he realized that the debates played some role. He hoped that scholars could study what impact they had and determine if

"It was the TV more than anything else that turned the tide."

As his wife, Jacqueline Bouvier Kennedy, looked on, Kennedy, the president-elect, prepared to speak.

they were worth doing again. Nixon also became convinced that having the candidates question each other on specific topics, with no journalists involved, would be a better format. He also believed each debate should be two hours, so the candidates could dig deeply into the issues.

Despite the popularity of the 1960 debates, some media experts and scholars were critical of them.

Charles Siepmann, a professor of communications in New York University's graduate progam, thought that some important issues were not covered in detail. He thought the candidates spent too much time talking about other issues, given the limited time they had. He also said that debating skills and looking good on television are not important qualities for a good president. Voters' judgment could be "warped," he wrote, by such things as "the mere matter of appearance . . . of ease of manner." Still, he admitted that drawing more people to watch the candidates and listen to their views was a good thing.

The issue of what kind of future debates to have, however, did not come up again for 16 years. The law that let the networks hold the 1960 debates applied only to that campaign. Also, in the presidential elections that followed, the Republican and Democratic candidates were not interested in taking part in debates. Before the 1964 presidential campaign began, Kennedy said he was interested in debating again. But Kennedy was assassinated on November 22, 1963. Vice President Lyndon Johnson then ran for president in 1964 and didn't talk about having debates. He was far ahead in the polls and didn't think he would gain anything from debating his Republican opponent, Barry Goldwater.

In 1968 Nixon ran for president again. His Democratic opponent, Hubert Humphrey, was ready

He also said that debating skills and looking good on television are not important qualities for a good president.

to debate, but Nixon said no. Some scholars were convinced that his experience in 1960 made him less than eager to debate again. Nixon won that campaign, and there were no debates when he ran for president again in 1972.

In the 1976 campaign, however, the two presidential candidates had more of a reason to want to debate. Nixon had resigned as president in 1974, as he faced possible impeachment in Congress.

Nixon's family stood with him as he resigned from the presidency on August 9, 1974.

His vice president, Gerald Ford, became president, and he pardoned Nixon for any crimes he might have committed while president. The pardon was not popular with many Americans. Early polls showed that Ford would have a tough time winning the presidential election. A debate in 1976 would give him a chance to make a good impression on voters. His opponent, Jimmy Carter, was also ready to debate. Carter's only political experience was serving as governor of Georgia, and he was not well-known across the country.

Before a debate could happen, however, the networks had to deal with the need to give candidates equal time, as outlined in Section 315 of the Communications Act. In 1975 the Federal Communications Commission settled the issue for good. The commission decided that Congress had not meant to apply the equal time requirement to debates. Showing debates on television was a valid part of covering the news, and news reports were not subject to Section 315. To qualify as news, the debates had to be between qualified candidates and be sponsored by an outside group, not the networks themselves.

In 1976, the League of Women Voters (LWV) agreed to sponsor debates between Ford and Carter. The LWV was founded in 1920, just before U.S. women won the right to vote. It did not support candidates from either party, but it encouraged people to take part in politics. The league asked

To qualify as news, the debates had to be between qualified candidates and be sponsored by an outside group, not the networks themselves.

Newton Minow to reach out to the candidates and begin making arrangements for the debates. Minow had once led the FCC, under President Kennedy.

The candidates quickly agreed to the idea of a debate, but as in 1960, they had to agree on the format. The LWV wanted to have at least three debates, including one in which the candidates directly questioned each other. But once again the candidates opposed this and wanted journalists to ask questions. Carter and Ford finally decided to hold three presidential debates. They also arranged for the first debate between vice presidential candidates—Walter Mondale, Carter's running mate, and Bob Dole, the Republican's vice presidential candidate.

Walter Cronkite, once the most trusted newsman in the U.S., led his network's coverage of the Ford-Carter debates.

As the debates approached in September 1976, reporters looked back to the first presidential debates of 1960. Some watched tapes of the Kennedy-Nixon debates to remind themselves how the candidates performed. *Washington Post* reporter Jules Witcover's impression was that Carter and Ford should focus on how they looked and sounded. That, and how they reacted to each other, would be more important than their ideas on the issues. Witcover wrote, "That is the one clear lesson that came through in the only previous televised presidential debates."

The second presidential debate began on September 23. Unlike the first, this time the two men appeared in front of a live audience of about 500 people. The evening went smoothly until, with just a few minutes left, the sound went dead. The two candidates waited almost half an hour for ABC, which was in charge of the production, to fix it. An estimated 70 million people watched the debate on television.

The Carter-Ford debates had two major differences from those in 1960. They were broadcast from public halls, not TV studios, in front of audiences. And after each one, reporters and experts went on TV to discuss what had been said and how the candidates did. In 1960 the networks had not offered these kinds of views after Nixon and Kennedy finished speaking. Actually, some of this kind of reporting began

For a time, the debate in 1980 between President Jimmy Carter and . . . Ronald Reagan was the most-watched TV broadcast in U.S. history.

because ABC lost the sound. The networks did not want the TV audience to sit through silence, so their newspeople began to talk about the debate, and in one case, a reporter asked a Ford aide how he thought the president was doing. "It's a clear-cut victory for the president so far," the aide said. This kind of praise from a candidate's team and supporters is known today as spin. The supporters want to shape how others will respond to what they just saw and heard in a way that favors their candidate. The comments from the reporters after the debate ended would come to be called instant analysis.

After 1976 presidential debates became a permanent part of U.S. politics. Candidates for other offices also sometimes held televised debates. But the ones for president always drew the most national attention. For a time, the debate in 1980 between President Jimmy Carter and Republican challenger Ronald Reagan was the most-watched TV broadcast in U.S. history. Almost 81 million people tuned in.

As in the past, each campaign season saw long negotiations on how to hold the debates. In 1980 the candidates wanted to have more say on which journalists took part. They thought some reporters might treat them unfairly. But the League of Women Voters thought that since it was running the debates, it should be able to choose which reporters it wanted.

Jimmy Carter (left) and Ronald Reagan squared off for Reagan's second presidential debate of 1980 and Carter's first.

In the end, though, it gave the candidates what they wanted. Newton Minow was still helping the league organize the debates. He didn't think the candidates should have all the control they sought. But the league had no way to force them to accept its rules. Minow later wrote, "The choice was to let the candidates call the shots or nothing—no debates."

THE MISSING CANDIDATE

Independent candidate John Anderson debated Ronald Reagan alone in the first presidential debate of 1980. It did not help his chances of winning.

The problems the League of Women Voters had in satisfying all the candidates in 1980 led to a first boycott. The league held presidential debates and the incumbent didn't attend. Along with Carter and Reagan, John Anderson was running as an independent. The league decided in September that Anderson was a serious enough candidate to be included in the first debate. He and Reagan agreed to take part, but Carter said he would attend only if he could debate Reagan alone first. The league said no, so Anderson and Reagan appeared together for an hour. The debate did not help Anderson in the polls, so the year's second debate included only Reagan and Carter. The news network CNN tried to include Anderson anyway, using videotapes of the real debate and inserting live clips of Anderson addressing the same questions the other two candidates did. The experiment, however, was a technical flop. Reagan went on to win the election.

1984 PRESIDENTIAL DEBATES

LEAGUE OF WOMEN VOT

Ronald Reagan and Walter Mondale had a spirited, but friendly, debate in 1984.

Some news companies refused to let their journalists take part in the 1980 debates, since they didn't like how the candidates were trying to control the process.

Relations between the league and the two major parties didn't improve after 1980. The league ran

the debates through the 1984 presidential election. That year Reagan was the incumbent and some of his supporters thought he should not debate his opponent, Democrat Walter Mondale. He was a popular president and didn't need the exposure on television. But Reagan thought the debates had become an important part of U.S. politics and should go on.

After that election, two studies of the presidential debates suggested that the Republican and Democratic parties should work together to set the ground rules for future debates. That led to the creation of the Commission on Presidential Debates (CPD) in 1987. The two parties supported it, but the commission was independent of both of them. Party leaders did not run the commission or set its rules. Money to run the commission came from the cities where the debates were held and from donations.

Since the creation of the CPD, presidential debates have experimented with various formats. A constant throughout their history has been enlisting a journalist to serve as moderator, just as Howard K. Smith did at the first Kennedy-Nixon debate. The moderator's role is to make sure the candidates follow the rules, especially on how much time they take to answer their questions. In some debates, the moderator has also been allowed to ask questions.

The 1992 debates saw a new format introduced— the town hall. During one debate, members of the audience were allowed to question the candidates.

President Bill Clinton (right) suggested a town hall format for his debate with Vice President George H.W. Bush. It highlighted his strengths and Bush's weaknesses.

The idea of town hall meetings was not new. New Englanders held the meetings during the 17th century so voters could discuss public issues and settle local affairs. The suggestion to have a more informal town hall format came from Democratic presidential candidate Bill Clinton. He had taken part in direct public meetings with groups of voters while serving as governor of Arkansas. He knew he connected well with the voters when he addressed them directly. President George H.W. Bush, who was running for reelection, went along with the idea.

For that first town hall debate in 1992, those two candidates and independent candidate Ross Perot took part. They met in front of a crowd of about 200 voters who said they had not yet decided who they wanted as president. Clinton followed Kennedy's example and prepared carefully. His aides set up a stage that showed where the other candidates, the cameras, and the audience would be. Clinton rehearsed on that stage, so he would know the best positions to be in when the real debate took place.

Afterward, a poll showed that voters enjoyed seeing regular Americans like themselves ask the candidates questions. Each presidential campaign since 1992 has featured one town hall debate. Since 2000, people wanting to ask questions have had to write them down first to avoid having similar questions asked. In 2008 people were allowed to submit some questions online before Senators Barack Obama and John McCain debated. In 2016, before the town hall, voters could submit questions online, and other Americans got to vote for the questions they wanted asked. Almost 4 million Americans voted. The top 30 questions were considered by CNN, the network hosting that debate.

By that debate, the Commission on Presidential Debates had clearly spelled out which candidates could take part in the debates. The candidates had to appear on the ballot in enough states to have a chance to win the 270 electoral votes needed to become president. In addition, five national opinion polls had to show that the candidate had the support of at least 15 percent of registered voters. The CPD said the rules would apply to anyone. Republican or Democratic candidates were not assured a spot at the debates simply because they belonged to one of the country's two major parties.

In the 21st century, voters have many more ways to watch the debates than they did in 1960. Along with the three broadcast networks of that day, many cable networks also televise the debates. Voters can also watch the debates live on the Internet. Many newspapers offer a live feed with commentary from reporters during the debate. The debates remain popular among viewers. In 2016 the total number of viewers for the three debates between Donald Trump and Hillary Clinton and the one between the vice presidential candidates was 259 million. That set a record for the total number of viewers for U.S. presidential debates. That figure was about 80 percent of the total population—below the 90 percent that saw or heard at least one Kennedy-Nixon debate.

Compared to many past debates, Trump and Clinton talked to each other more than previous candidates had. During their first debate, they took questions only from the moderator, Lester Holt. At one point, each asked viewers to look at their campaign websites to check facts. The Internet was allowing

Hillary Clinton (right) and Donald J. Trump engaged in very heated debates in 2016.

voters to be more involved in the process than ever before. And thanks to social media, viewers can see what experts think of the debates while they are still happening. They can also share their own opinions with millions of people.

While voters and TV networks like the presidential debates, some experts still have questions about them. They worry that the debates put too much attention on how candidates look and act rather than if they are qualified to be president. The critics say the debates have become more like entertainment and less about political issues. Kathleen Hall Jamieson, a professor at the University of Pennsylvania, has studied the debates. In 2015 Jamieson said the entertainment part of debates is not necessarily bad. "The question is, do we get some substantive discussion?" But even without a deep probing of the issues, Jamieson says, voters get a sense of who the candidates are as people.

Today, discussions of the presidential debate still steer people back to the first ones in 1960. Viewers can watch all four on the Internet and see for themselves how Kennedy and Nixon looked, talked, and acted on TV. Their debates made history and shaped U.S. politics. Journalist Russell Baker, who covered the 1960 campaign, wrote this decades after the first Great Debate: "That night, television replaced newspapers as the most important communications medium in American politics."

"That night, television replaced newspapers as the most important communications medium in American politics."

HIGHLIGHTS OF THE PRESIDENTIAL DEBATES

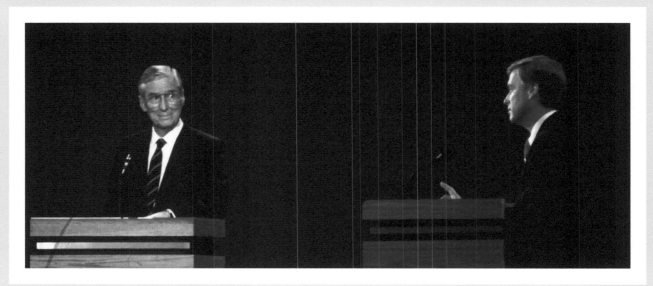

In the 1988 vice presidential debate, Democrat Lloyd Bentsen (left) shot off one of the most memorable lines of all time.

The debates since 1976 have led to some memorable moments in U.S. politics. Candidates have made mistakes that hurt their campaign or said lines that people remembered long after the debate was over. Here are some examples.

1976: Gerald Ford said that Poland and other communist nations in Eastern Europe were not under the control of the Soviet Union. As president, he should have known that in fact the Soviets did heavily control the governments in those countries.

1980: When President Carter made a comment that Ronald Reagan disagreed with, Reagan said, "There you go again." He meant to suggest that Carter had often not accurately described Reagan's views or actions.

1984: Running for reelection against Democrat Walter Mondale, Reagan once again delivered a memorable line. Reagan knew that some Americans wondered if, at 73, he was too old for the job. But before Mondale could make Reagan's age an issue, the president joked, "I will not make age an issue of this campaign. I am not going to exploit, for political purposes, my opponent's youth and inexperience."

1988: In the vice presidential debate, Republican candidate Dan Quayle seemed to compare his experience to John Kennedy's before he became president. His opponent, Lloyd Bentsen, shot back, "I served with Jack Kennedy. I knew Jack Kennedy. Jack Kennedy was a friend of mine. Senator, you are no Jack Kennedy."

1988: In the presidential debates, Democratic candidate Michael Dukakis turned off some voters when he showed no emotion when a panelist asked if he would favor the death penalty for someone who had raped and murdered his wife. Dukakis simply stated his long-held beliefs against the death penalty.

2016: In a race that often drew sharp comments from both presidential candidates, Hillary Clinton tried to show that she was ready to be president and Donald Trump was not. In their first debate, she said, "I think Donald just criticized me for preparing for this debate. And, yes, I did. You know what else I prepared for? I prepared to be president. And I think that's a good thing." Clinton also pointed out harsh comments Trump had made in the past about women. Trump claimed he never made the comments and said he could have made "rough" comments about Clinton and her family, but "it's not nice." At the end of the last debate, though, he called her "such a nasty woman."

Timeline

1858

Abraham Lincoln and Stephen Douglas hold a series of debates in Illinois—the most famous U.S. political debates before 1960

1924

Political conventions are broadcast on radio for the first time

1952

Political conventions are broadcast on TV for the first time; Richard Nixon gives his Checkers speech on television; Senator Blair Moody makes the first public call for televised debates between the presidential candidates

1933

President Franklin D. Roosevelt gives his first Fireside Chat over radio

1940

President Franklin D. Roosevelt refuses a challenge from Wendell Wilkie to debate on radio

1956

Adlai Stevenson and Estes Kefauver hold a debate that is televised across the country; John F. Kennedy gives his first national TV speech during the Democratic Convention

1960

Congress makes a one-time exception to a broadcasting law to let Kennedy and Nixon take part in presidential debates; Kennedy gives a televised speech saying his Roman Catholic beliefs would not affect his presidency; on September 26, Kennedy and Nixon hold the first of four televised debates, the first ever between two presidential candidates; Kennedy wins the election

Timeline

1975

A ruling by the FCC makes it possible for TV networks to broadcast political debates if certain rules are met

1976

Gerald Ford and Jimmy Carter take part in the first presidential debates since 1960; the first vice presidential debate is held

1992

The first town hall debate takes place between President George H.W. Bush, Bill Clinton, and Ross Perot

2008

Voters are allowed to submit questions online for the town hall debate between Barack Obama and John McCain

1980

President Jimmy Carter refuses to take part in one debate because it includes an independent candidate, John Anderson

1987

The Commission on Presidential Debates is formed to oversee how the debates are run

2016

The three presidential debates and one vice presidential debate draw a record number of viewers

Glossary

administration—group of officials who work for a president

airtime—period that a program is broadcast over TV or radio

ballot—list of candidates voters choose from

campaigning—seeking support from voters through public appearances and the media

candidates—people running for a political office

communism—form of government that restricts personal freedom and allows only one political party

contrast—difference between the lightest and darkest parts of an image

convention—meeting held by political parties to choose their candidates

domestic—relating to the political issues inside a particular country

incumbent—the person currently holding a political office

innovation—a new idea or device

impeachment—a political process to remove a government official who is accused of breaking the law

nomination—the act of choosing a particular person to represent a party for a specific office

regulate—control in a way that prevents unlawful or harmful behavior

split-screen—TV image cut in half to show two different pictures at once

ticket—the candidates from one political party during an election

transcript—an exact printed record of what someone has spoken at a particular event

Additional Resources

Further Reading

Anderson, Holly Lynn. *The Presidential Election Process*. Pittsburgh: Eldorado Ink, 2016.

Chandler, Julia. *Richard Nixon*. New York: Britannica Educational Publishing, 2017.

Collins, Anne. *John F. Kennedy*. Oxford: Oxford University Press, 2014.

Morris-Lipsman. *Presidential Races: Campaigning for the White House* (Revised Edition). Minneapolis, Minn.: Twenty-First Century Books, 2012.

Internet Sites

Use FactHound to find Internet sites related to this book.
Visit *www.facthound.com*
Just type in 9780756558239 and go.

Critical Thinking Questions

Scholars disagree on how much the TV debates influenced the outcome of the 1960 elections. Using examples from the text, explain whether you think they made a difference, and why.

Before he debated Vice President George H.W. Bush, Democratic candidate Bill Clinton followed John F. Kennedy's lead in preparation. Why do you think he did so? Did it have any effect?

Debaters have gotten more combative in recent years. Do you think that helps or hurts voters' ability to choose the right candidate for president?

Source Notes

p. 4, "A brutal schedule..." Richard M. Nixon. *Six Crises*. Garden City, N.Y.: Doubleday & Company, 1962, p. 329.

p. 5, "How do you feel?" Alan Schroeder. *Presidential Debates: Risky Business on the Campaign Trail, 3rd ed.* New York: Columbia University Press, 2016, p. 2.

p. 8, "The church does not speak for me..." Transcript: JFK's Speech on His Religion, NPR, December 5, 2007, http://www.npr.org/templates/story/story.php?storyId=16920600. Accessed on September 30, 2017.

p. 10, "Is definitely an asset..." Thomas Oliphant and Curtis Wilkie. *The Road to Camelot: Inside JFK's Five-Year Campaign.* New York: Simon & Schuster, 2017, p. 294.

p. 11, "I just want to says..." Address of Senator Nixon to the American People: The 'Checkers Speech,' September 23, 1952. Accessed on September 15, 2017.

p. 12, "I would have opened myself..." Nixon. *Six Crises*, p. 323.

p. 13, "He wanted to know everything..." G. Scott Thomas. *A New World to Be Won: John Kennedy, Richard Nixon, and the Tumultuous Year of 1960.* Santa Barbara, CA: Praeger, 2011, p. 210.

p. 14, "Would be peeled down to the man himself..." Austin C. Wehrwein, "Nominees Agreed on Debate's Value; Final Preparations Are Made by C.B.S. for Tomorrow's Domestic Issues Panel." *New York Times*, September 25, 1960, p. 56.

p. 19, "If there were more of them..." Sidney Kraus, ed., *The Great Debates: Kennedy vs. Nixon, 1960.* Bloomington: Indiana University Press, 1977, p. 40.

p. 21, "An electronic innovation..." Jack Gould, "TV: Political Politeness; Kefauver and Stevenson Have Informal Chat on Subdued A.B.C. Program," *New York Times*, May 22, 1956, p. 67.

"p. 27, Nixon probably lost the debate..." W.J. Rorabaugh. *The Real Making of the President: Kennedy, Nixon, and the 1960 Election.*

Lawrence: University Press of Kansas, 2009, p. 151.

p. 28, "In the direction of slavery..." 1960 Debates, Commission on Presidential Debates, http://www.debates.org/index.php?page=1960-debates Accessed on October 7, 2017.

p. 30, "Very useful" W.H. Lawrence, "Neither Nominee Claims a Triumph; Both Are Satisfied With TV Debate and Feel Voters Will Render Decision," *New York Times*, September 27, 1960, p 30.

p. 31, "Had given him a star quality..." Schroeder. *Presidential Debates*, p. 9.

p. 31, "I heard so much about Kennedy" Kraus. *The Great Debates*, p. 158.

p. 32, "Was on top of his subject..." Thomas. *A New World*, p. 212.

p. 32, "I should have remembered..." Nixon. *Six Crises*, p. 340.

p. 33, "Boy, did I nail him" Rorabaugh. *Real Making of the President*, p. 154.

p. 33, "Real discussion..." Newton N. Minow and Craig L. LaMay. *Inside the Presidential Debates: Their Improbable Past and Promising Future.* Chicago: University of Chicago Press, 2008, p. 13.

p. 33, "The presence of both candidates..." Jack Gould, "TV: The Great Debate; First Nixon and Kennedy Discussion Is Called a Constructive Innovation," *New York Times*, September 27, 1960, p. 75.

p. 33, "But they both handled themselves well..." Kraus. *The Great Debates*, p. 151.

p. 33, "A brilliant lesson..." Minow and LaMay. *Inside the Presidential Debates*, p. 14.

p. 34, "The Vice President clearly won..." Nixon, *Six Crises*, p. 344.

p. 38, "It was the TV..." Kayla Webley, "How the Nixon-Kennedy Debate Changed the World," *Time*, September 23, 2010, http://content.time.com/time/nation/article/0,8599,2021078,00.html Accessed on September 6, 2017.

p. 40, "Warped..." Kraus. *The Great Debates*, p. 137.

p. 44, "one clear lesson..." Schroeder. *Presidential Debates*, p. 118.

p. 45, "It's a clear-cut victory..." Ibid., p. 295.

p. 54, "The question is..." Joseph P. Williams, "Do Debates Matter?" *U.S. News & World Report*, November 13, 2015, https://www.usnews.com/news/the-report/articles/2015/11/13/do-presidential-debates-matter Accessed on October 13, 2017.

p. 54, "That night, television replaced newspapers..." Schroeder. *Presidential Debates*, p. 295.

p. 55, "There you go again..." Kenneth T. Walsh, "6 Best 'Zingers' From Past Presidential Debates," *U.S. News & World Report*, October 1, 2012, https://www.usnews.com/news/blogs/ken-walshs-washington/2012/10/01/6-best-zingers-from-past-presidential-debates Accessed on October 14, 2017.

p. 55, "I will not make age an issue..." "Transcript of the Reagan-Mondale Debate on Foreign Policy," *New York Times*, October 22, 1984. http://www.nytimes.com/1984/10/22/us/transcript-of-the-reagan-mondale-debate-on-foreign-policy.html?pagewanted=all Accessed on December 3, 2017.

p. 55, "I served with Jack Kennedy..." "6 Best 'Zingers' From Past Presidential Debates."

p. 55, "I think Donald just criticized me..." Aaron Blake, "The First Trump-Clinton Presidential Debate Transcript, Annotated, *Washington Post*, September 26, 2016, https://www.washingtonpost.com/news/the-fix/wp/2016/09/26/the-first-trump-clinton-presidential-debate-transcript-annotated/?utm_term=.6a78da2dd727 Accessed on December 3, 2017.

p. 55, "Rough..." "It's not nice..." Ibid.

p. 55, "Such a nasty woman..." Full transcript: Third 2016 Presidential Debate, *Politico*, October 20, 2016, http://www.politico.com/story/2016/10/full-transcript-third-2016-presidential-debate-230063 Accessed on October 14, 2017.

Select Bibliography

Books

Kraus, Sidney, ed. *The Great Debates: Kennedy vs. Nixon, 1960.* Bloomington: Indiana University Press, 1977.

Minow, Newton N., and Craig L. LaMay. *Inside the Presidential Debates: Their Improbable Past and Promising Future.* Chicago: University of Chicago Press, 2008.

Nixon, Richard M. *Six Crises.* Garden City, N.Y.: Doubleday & Company, 1962.

Rorabaugh, W.J. *The Real Making of the President: Kennedy, Nixon, and the 1960 Election.* Lawrence: University Press of Kansas, 2009.

Schroeder, Alan. *Presidential Debates: Risky Business on the Campaign Trail. 3rd ed.* New York: Columbia University Press, 2016.

Self, John W. *Presidential Debate Negotiation from 1960 to 1988: Setting the Stage for Prime-Time Clashes.* Lanham, MD: Lexington Books, 2016.

Thomas, G. Scott. *A New World to Be Won: John Kennedy, Richard Nixon, and the Tumultuous Year of 1960.* Santa Barbara, CA: Praeger, 2011.

Websites and Articles

Allen, Erika Tyner. "The Kennedy-Nixon Presidential Debates, 1960." Archive of American Television. http://www.emmytvlegends.org/interviews/kennedy-nixon-debates# Accessed on September 12, 2017.

Bingham, Amy. "Nixon Admits 1960 Debate Prep Was 'Totally Wrong.'" ABC News, October 3, 2012. http://abcnews.go.com/blogs/politics/2012/10/nixon-admits-1960-debate-prep-was-totally-wrong/ Accessed on October 5, 2017.

Gidlow, Liette. "The Great Debate: Kennedy, Nixon and Television in the 1960 Race for the Presidency." *History Now*, the Journal of the Gilder Lehrman Institute. https://www.gilderlehrman.org/history-by-era/sixties/essays/great-debate-kennedy-nixon-and-television-1960-race-for-presidency Accessed on September 6, 2017.

Greenberg, David. "Rewinding the Kennedy-Nixon Debates: Did JFK Really Win Because He Looked Better on Television?" *Slate*, September 24, 2010. http://www.slate.com/articles/news_and_politics/history_lesson/2010/09/rewinding_the_kennedynixon_debates.2.html Accessed on September 20, 2017.

Kirkpatrick, Dan. "The Political Broadcasting Rules: A Refresher Course." CommLawBlog, November 8, 2015. http://www.commlawblog.com/2015/11/articles/broadcast/the-political-broadcasting-rules-a-refresher-course/ Accessed on October 10, 2017.

Lawrence, W.H. "Neither Nominee Claims a Triumph; Both Are Satisfied With TV Debate and Feel Voters Will Render Decision." *New York Times*, September 27, 1960, p.Tra 30.

Levy, Angelia. "Media Myth Surrounding the 1960 Kennedy-Nixon Presidential Debates & the Boston Globe." You're Entitled to Be Wrong, May 9, 2010. https://angelialevy.com/2010/05/09/media-myth-surrounding-the-1960-kennedy-nixon-presidential-debates/ Accessed on October 8, 2017.

Mazzo, Earl. "The Great Debates." The History of Televised Presidential Debates. http://www.museum.tv/debateweb/html/greatdebate/e_mazzo.htm Accessed on September 15, 2017.

McCartney, Robert. "How a Bethesda Retiree Altered 1960 Debates. Commission on Presidential Debates. http://www.debates.org/index.php?page=1960-debates Accessed on October 7, 2017.

"Radio: A Consumer Product and a Producer of Consumption." Coolidge-Consumerism Collection, Library of Congress. http://lcweb2.loc.gov:8081/ammem/amrlhtml/inradio.html Accessed on October 3. 2017.

"10 Famous Political Debate Moments." National Constitution Center, September 26, 2016. https://constitutioncenter.org/blog/10-famous-political-debate-moments/ Accessed on September 12, 2016.

"Transcript of the Reagan-Mondale Debate on Foreign Policy," *New York Times*, October 22, 1984. http://www.nytimes.com/1984/10/22/us/transcript-of-the-reagan-mondale-debate-on-foreign-policy.html?pagewanted=all Accessed on December 3, 2017.

Voter Turnout in Presidential Elections: 1828 – 2012. The American Presidency Project.

Walsh, Kenneth T. "6 Best 'Zingers' From Past Presidential Debates." *U.S. News & World Report*, October 1, 2012. https://www.usnews.com/news/blogs/ken-walshs-washington/2012/10/01/6-best-zingers-from-past-presidential-debates Accessed on October 14, 2017.

Webley, Kayla. "How the Nixon-Kennedy Debate Changed the World." *Time*, September 23, 2010. http://content.time.com/time/nation/article/0,8599,2021078,00.html Accessed on September 6, 2017.

Williams, Joseph P. "Do Debates Matter?" *U.S. News & World Report*, November 13, 2015. https://www.usnews.com/news/the-report/articles/2015/11/13/do-presidential-debates-matter Accessed on October 13, 2017.

Wooten, James T. "Sound of Debate Is Off Air for 27 Minutes." *New York Times*, September 24, 1976. http://www.nytimes.com/1976/09/24/archives/sound-of-debate-is-off-air-for-27-minutes-debates-sound-goes-off.html Accessed on October 12, 2017.

Index

About the Author

Michael Burgan has written many books for children and young adults during his 20 years as a freelance writer. Most of his books have focused on history. Burgan has won several awards for his writing. He lives in Santa Fe, New Mexico.